THE MYSTERY OF
STONEHENGE

THE MYSTERY OF
STONEHENGE

FRANKLYN M. BRANLEY
Illustrated by Victor G. Ambrus

THOMAS Y. CROWELL COMPANY, NEW YORK

DESIGNED BY JUDIE MILLS

Manufactured in the United States of America

L. C. Card 69-11823

1   2   3   4   5   6   7   8   9   10

BY THE AUTHOR

The Christmas Sky
Experiments in Sky Watching
The Mystery of Stonehenge
The Nine Planets

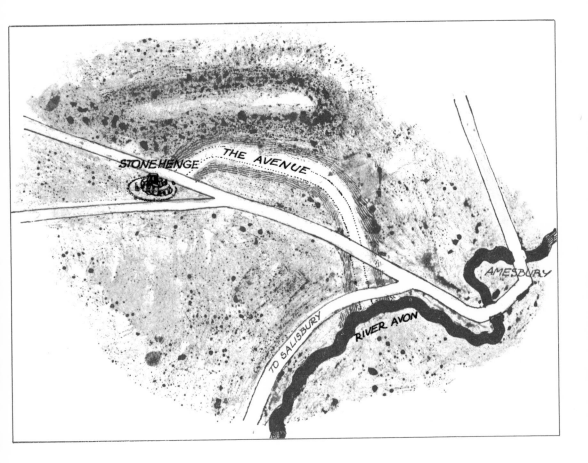

THE MYSTERY OF
STONEHENGE

For hundreds of years men have wondered about Stonehenge. They have studied the great circle of huge stone pillars—some standing erect, others lying on the ground where they fell centuries ago.

Stonemasons wonder how the stones were cut and shaped.

Engineers wonder how the stones—some weighing many tons— were hauled to this place and set upright.

Archeologists wonder about the bronze daggers, blue and amber beads, bits of pottery, and crude tools that they have found around Stonehenge. They wonder about the people who made these things.

Anthropologists, too, wonder about the people. How did they live? Were they peaceful or warlike? Did they hunt for most of their food, or were they farmers? Modern investigators wonder why the Stonehenge people did not survive—or if they did survive, why they moved away.

Engineers, anthropologists, archeologists, astronomers, and other scientists (and nonscientists, too) wonder about the most challenging riddle of all: Why was Stonehenge built? What was its purpose?

The word Stonehenge means "the hanging stones." We do not know who gave the place this name, but it is a good one. Some of the stone pillars still stand, just as they did 4,000 years ago. Across the tops of a few of the pillars, connecting one to another, are smaller stones that seem to "hang" in space.

This place of the hanging stones stands on a rise in a wide, rolling plain near Salisbury, England. Why is Stonehenge located at this lonely place? This is one of the mysteries that have never been solved. Nor do we know how Stonehenge was built. How were the stones brought here? Where did they come from? How were they set upright, and how were the smaller stones placed atop the high, massive pillars?

These are more of the mysteries of Stonehenge. Perhaps we shall never know the answers to them. But the archeologists, anthropologists, and engineers who have studied this monument have developed theories about how it may have been built.

The outer ring of stones at Stonehenge was made of 30 massive pillars, some of them weighing as much as 40 tons. No stones like these can be found anywhere else on the surrounding plain.

They probably came from a quarry that is located 24 miles away. The stones had to be hauled over this distance by the men building Stonehenge. Then they had to be cut into shape and set in place. After that the smaller stones, called lintels, were set on top of them.

The builders of Stonehenge must have moved the huge stones overland. Yet they had no horses to pull them. They had no carts, nor did they have wheels.

One theory of how the men of Stonehenge hauled the stones and set them in place suggests that sledges were built from heavy

logs. Perhaps the logs were tied together with ropes made from the skins of animals. Or the sledges may have been little more than the forks from large, heavy trees, dragged along the ground with the stones resting upon them.

Scores of men helped to push and pull the heavy stones onto the sledges. Long ropes were fastened to each stone, and teams of men pulled while others pushed. One time, by accident, a sledge may have been pulled up onto a log. As the men pulled, the log rolled, and the sledge moved more easily. And so the men building Stonehenge may have learned to use rollers.

There may have been some teams of men whose job it was to put rollers in front of the sledge. According to this theory, as the sledge was pulled along, the men transferred the rollers from back to front. And so there grew a continuous roadway of rollers to make the task easier.

Some scientists think that the builders may have moved the stones only during winter. When the ground was covered with snow and ice, the sledges would have slid along quite easily. Teams of men holding control ropes would have been needed to keep the sledges from sliding to one side, or from speeding down-hill and crushing the hauling teams.

Archeologists think that 800 men would have been needed to haul the stones. It would have taken 200 more men to move the rollers and to keep the heavy stone blocks from sliding. The task must have required many years to complete.

Within the main circle of pillars at Stonehenge is another ring of smaller stones that weigh about 5 tons each. These are of a different type of rock from the large pillars. They are called blue-stones, because of their coloration. Stones like these can be found no nearer than about 250 miles from the Salisbury Plain.

Scientists think that expeditions of Stonehenge men searched for these special stones because they were thought to contain mystic qualities. Moving them over 250 miles must have been very difficult. They may have been floated on rafts for a part of this distance, or drawn through the water hung between dugout canoes or boats made of animal skins. But they had to be hauled overland at least part of the way, perhaps on sledges. When the Avon River, which flows through the Salisbury Plain, was reached, the stones were probably loaded onto rafts and floated to within 2 miles of the site of Stonehenge.

Both the tall stone pillars and the smaller bluestones were shaped by human effort. Some of them are squared off, and some are tapered or rounded. The stones are shaped—yet Stonehenge was built before metal tools were used in England. The men probably used smaller stones, weighing up to 60 pounds, to bash the large pillars and chip them, hoping the breaks would occur in the right places. To increase the chances of splitting the stones as desired, fire was probably used.

With a hard, sharp rock, a line would first be scratched across a stone where the men wanted it to break. Then fires were kindled along this line—perhaps by laying cattails soaked in animal fat on the stone and then setting them on fire. When the stone was hot, the ashes would be brushed away, and cold water splashed along the line. Possibly heavy boulders were dropped on the hot stone at the same time. The large stones might then have split because of the sudden change in temperature—or large chips

might have broken free. The process would have had to be repeated over and over again, until the stone split through.

Large stones also were broken into smaller ones by using stone and wooden wedges. The stone wedges would be pounded into a crack, forcing it open. Wooden wedges were probably forced into the crack, and water was poured over the wood, making it swell. As the wood expanded, it would split the rock. Maybe the crack was just a little bit wider at first—but after the operation was repeated again and again, the rock would finally be split through.

Rough shaping of the stones was probably done at the place where they were found. After the stones were brought to the Salisbury Plain, the shaping was completed. Months of pounding were needed to square off each stone. Sometimes the rough edges were removed, and the surfaces were smoothed by grinding. To grind the stones, one stone was pushed and pulled back and forth across another one. Particles of hard stone, as small as grains of sand, were mixed with water to make a grinding compound that was spread between the two surfaces.

The tops of the main pillars are not flat. Each has a knoblike projection, about 8 inches across and 3 inches high, which fits into a hollow that was ground out of the corresponding lintel stone. Carpenters today use the same idea to make a strong joint, called a mortise and tenon.

The stones were dragged to Stonehenge from far-off places. This took hundreds of men, hard labor, and many years. After being pounded, shaped, and ground, the stones had to be set in place. Holes 8 feet deep were dug. Stonehenge men used flat stones, animal bones, and deer antlers to loosen the soil. Three sides of each hole were straight up and down. The fourth side was slanted. The side of the hole opposite this sloped side was lined with timbers. A pillar was hauled to the site and positioned so that one end projected over the slanting side of the hole. The other end was then raised by pushing logs under it, until the stone slid down into the hole. When the stone hit the opposite side, the timbers kept the wall from caving in.

Lines made from vines and the skins of animals were fastened to a collar, made of logs and leather belts, that was wrapped around the upper end of the pillar. By pulling on the lines and pushing on the collar with long poles, the men eased the stone to an upright position. Once in place, it was held steady while dozens of men filled in the hole as fast as they could with soil, stones, logs, wood chips, and whatever else they could get hold of quickly.

The upright stones took weeks to settle into place. The tops of each pair of stones had to be chipped and ground down to make one level with the other. Then the heavy lintel stones were placed on top of them. These crosspieces may have been pushed up a ramp made from rocks and soil.

Some archeologists, who have been especially interested in the engineering problems of ancient peoples, think that no ramp at all was used. They believe that the lintel was first placed against one of the upright stones. Logs were then laid alongside the lintel, and the lintel stone was rocked onto the logs. More logs were laid down to fill the space between the pillar and the lintel, which now rested on a log layer. Next, the lintel was inched over onto these logs, back against the side of the pillar. Then another layer of logs was put in place. This process of building a layer, moving the lintel onto it, then building another layer alongside, continued until the lintel rested on a tower of logs that was level with the tops of the two stone pillars. Finally, according to the theory, the lintel was eased over so that the mortises (the depressions in the lintel) fitted onto the tenons on the top of each pillar. Perhaps the mortises were ground into the lintels after they were on top of the log towers.

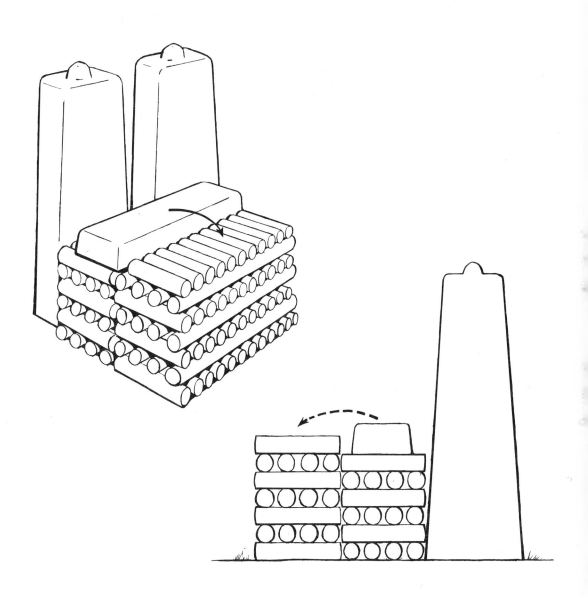

Some people have figured that 250 logs, each 20 feet long and 6 inches across, would be needed to build the tower. Each log would have to be notched so it would fit into crossbars, to keep it from slipping. Cutting and notching so many logs using nothing but stone axes would be a hard job all by itself. Erecting the stone pillars and raising the lintels must have been major tasks.

Maybe the pillars were hauled to the Salisbury Plain on sledges —and maybe they were shaped and erected in the ways described above. Or the work may have been accomplished in ways no one has considered. How Stonehenge was actually built may remain a mystery forever. Certainly scientists have very few clues to help them find the solution.

When Stonehenge was built is another mystery—although part of the answer has been found.

Archeologists have dug carefully around the stones of Stonehenge, and they have also excavated large areas of the Salisbury Plain. As they dug, the scientists came across bits of charcoal buried in the ground—charcoal left from the ashes of fires that burned centuries ago.

A small pinch of charcoal is all that the archeologist needs to find out how many years ago the wood was put on the fire. The process of finding the age of burnt wood and animal bone is called radiocarbon dating. This is the way it is done:

Plants take in carbon dioxide from the air. There are two kinds of carbon in this substance—carbon 12 and carbon 14. When the plant is alive, it has one carbon 14 atom for every trillion carbon 12 atoms it contains. As long as the plant lives, these relative amounts of carbon 12 and carbon 14 remain the same. But when the plant dies, the amount of carbon 14 starts to dwindle, while the amount of carbon 12 does not change. That happens because the carbon 14 atoms are radioactive—they change to nitrogen, and are not replaced.

Scientists know that one half of the carbon 14 atoms in the dead plant material will change to nitrogen every 5,760 years. So, to find the age of a piece of charcoal (which is the remains of a plant), the scientist determines the relative amounts of carbon

12 and carbon 14 that are in the sample. Once he knows these, he can figure out its age. For example:

Suppose that when the plant was alive it had 100 trillion atoms of carbon 12. It would therefore have had 100 atoms of carbon 14. If a scientist, in examining the charcoal from the ancient fire, found only 50 atoms of carbon 14 for the 100 trillion atoms of carbon 12, he would know that the charcoal was 5,760 years old. Similarly, if he found only 25 carbon 14 atoms, the charcoal would be twice that old—or 11,520 years old.

By testing the charcoal found at Stonehenge, archeologists have learned that it comes from wood that grew 3,700 years ago. Since the construction of Stonehenge probably occurred at the same time that the fires were burned, it seems that the monument was built around 1800 B.C. That was at the end of the Stone Age in England —before metal tools were used in that part of the world. We are quite certain about the time Stonehenge was built, because radio-carbon tests are highly accurate.

But not all of Stonehenge was built at the same time. Archeologists are quite sure about this, because in their digging they have found the ashes of fires on top of the ashes of other fires. The ones underneath must have been built earlier.

The first part of Stonehenge to be completed was probably a ring-shaped ditch. This circle is about 300 feet across. As men dug the ditch they piled the soil along the rim, and so a mound was made. The 56 holes just inside the mound were probably dug at the same time.

Two hundred years or so later, the second stage—the bluestone circle—was built. It was set near the center of the large ring. (The bluestones are those that were hauled 250 miles.) Only a few of the stones now stand; most have fallen over or have been removed. We know the bluestones must have been put there after the ditch was dug, because of bits of broken pottery unearthed near the bluestones. The pottery was produced around 1600 B.C., according to radiocarbon dating methods—200 years after the ditch was made.

A broad avenue, visible today as a slight depression in the land with mounds on either side, stretches from Stonehenge across the Salisbury Plain to the Avon River. Some archeologists think that this was the entrance to Stonehenge, and that it was built at the same time the bluestones were erected.

A hundred years or more went by before the large stone pillars were added, and their lintels set in place. Thus, at least 300 years were required to complete Stonehenge.

The efforts of thousands of people, spread over several generations, went into the building of Stonehenge. No one is certain who these people were, or where they came from.

Anthropologists know that there were large numbers of people in Stone Age England. But they cannot isolate any single group and say that these were the people who built Stonehenge. One clue, however, excites investigators, because it may point toward an answer. Imprints of short daggers, with handles and crossbars, have been found on the sides of some of the stone pillars. The dagger has a peculiar shape that identifies it as the same type used by the Myceneans—a people who lived in ancient Greece. A few archeologists think that expeditions from Greece may have traveled over sea and land to England. Once there, they may have remained 300 years or so—long enough to build Stonehenge.

Maybe the Myceneans did build the monument—but more likely it was built by men who knew nothing about metals and metalworking. Perhaps we shall never know for sure. To find out, a thorough investigation of Stonehenge, including deep digging, would have to be made. But even this extensive digging might not provide any further clues. And unfortunately Stonehenge can never be excavated, because all the stones would have to be removed. Digging in the central part of the site is prohibited for fear the stones now standing might fall and shatter.

Today Stonehenge is an awesome ruin. Four thousand years ago it must have been a monument of great importance. Generations of men dedicated their lives to hauling the stones, shaping them, and setting them into precise positions in their plan for the site.

Stonehenge may have been a religious temple—a dwelling place of the gods. Men of the Stone Age may have made pilgrimages to the monument, approaching it from the nearby Avon River. They would have seen the pillars stark against the skyline as they stepped into the broad avenue that spans the distance from the river to the impressive circles of stone. Mounds and ditches on both sides would have directed their steps along the avenue.

Two miles from the river, the men would have arrived at a giant boulder, set solidly in the ground and rising to a height of 12 feet. This solitary sentinel is now called the Heel Stone—probably because of a legend well known in the region. According to the story, a certain monk who lived near Salisbury made the Devil very angry. The Devil, consequently, picked up this huge boulder and threw it at the monk, hitting him on the heel. But the monk was so strong and hard that the stone did not hurt him at all. Rather, the stone was broken by his heel. Today a large nick near the base of the stone is proof enough for some people that the legend is true.

Proceeding beyond the Heel Stone, men of the Stone Age would have passed between two more stones set upright, serving as a gateway or entrance to the ring of ditches and mounds. Today only one of these stones remains, and it has fallen to the ground. It is called the Slaughter Stone—probably because modern men have imagined that it marked a place used for making offerings to pagan gods.

Now the men would be close enough to be awed and astounded by the enormous pillars. To reach them, they had to cross a mound and a ditch. Beyond this are three separate rings of holes, one ring inside another. Through the centuries these holes have been

filled in by the limestone of the plain itself. The 56 holes in the outer ring are called Aubrey Holes, after the anthropologist who dug into them 300 years ago. They originally were each about 3 feet across and 2 feet deep. When Aubrey and other scientists after him dug into the holes, they found human bones in some of them, along with bones of animals, crude tools, and pottery. Some think the holes were disposal areas or burial places.

Within the ring of Aubrey Holes are two more rings of small holes. No one knows what their purpose may have been. Maybe small stone pillars were placed in them at one time. Today the holes are little more than slight depressions in the ground.

Seventeen gigantic stone pillars now stand within the rings of holes. When Stonehenge was built, there were 30 pillars. Some have fallen; others have been removed. The pillars are known as monoliths, or single stones. The distance from the center of one stone to the center of the next is 10 feet. Each is 7 feet wide and $13\frac{1}{2}$ feet above the ground.

Today people call the pillars the Sarsen Stones. Together they form the Sarsen Circle. We don't know why that name is used— though some say the word "Sarsen" comes from "Saracen." The Saracens were nomadic tribes who pillaged towns and villages, and so the word Saracen (Sarsen) is often used to refer to anything that is primitive, rough, or pagan.

The 30 pillars were joined together in pairs by the large stones laid across their tops. These are the lintel stones (or simply lintels). Six of them remain in position. They were cut to a curve to fit the circle. Most of the lintels have fallen, and lie on the ground. Others have disappeared. They may have been used years ago for building stones by farmers of the region.

Within the outer circle of pillars is the bluestone ring. The bluestones are smaller than the Sarsens. They are worn quite smooth and have rounded edges. Today there are 20 stones in the bluestone ring. Some of them stand upright, much as they did originally, while others have fallen. From the drawing you can see that there are gaps in the circle—places where there are no stones at all. In some of the blank areas, stumps of stones have been located under the ground. The stones were probably broken off.

The giants of Stonehenge stand at the center of the monument, arranged in a horseshoe pattern. On one side of the horseshoe, two pillars tower 20 feet above the ground. Each stone is almost 30 feet from end to end, counting the part that is sunk under the ground. A lintel stone rests on top of the pillars, arching from one to the other.

Two more giants stand on the other side—also topped by a lintel stone. At the bend of the horseshoe stands the tallest of all

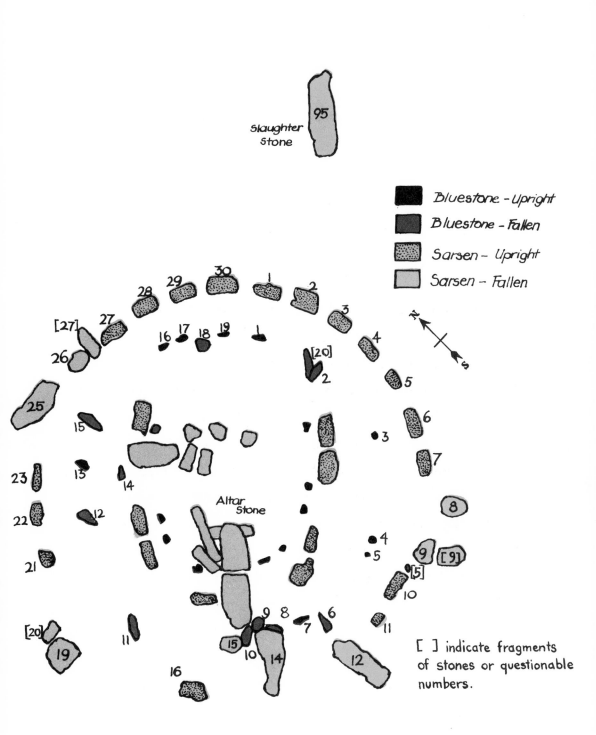

Slaughter Stone

95

Bluestone – Upright
Bluestone – Fallen
Sarsen – Upright
Sarsen – Fallen

30 29 28 1 2
[27] 27 26 16 17 18 19 1 3
25 15 4
23 15 14 [20] 2 5
22 12 Altar Stone 3 6
21 14 4 7
[20] 19 11 16 9 8 7 6 8
15 10 14 5 9 [9]
12 [5] 10 11

[ ] indicate fragments
of stones or questionable
numbers.

the stones of Stonehenge. It rises 25 feet above the ground. At its top, one can see clearly the tenon upon which a lintel rested at one time. Another giant stone once stood here beside it, but it has fallen and broken in two. The lintel that joined these two huge pillars has also fallen.

Near the open end of the horseshoe is another pair of mammoth pillars topped by a lintel. These stones are slightly smaller than those at the bend of the horseshoe. Just opposite these three stones, at the other end, is a single stone. Alongside it on the ground are the broken pieces of the pillar that once stood beside it, and of the lintel stone that joined them.

Each group of three stones—the two upright pillars and the lintel that spans their tops—is called a trilithon. The opening between each pair of pillars is only about 12 inches wide.

Within the horseshoe of giant trilithons are a group of stones only a few feet high—again arranged in a crude horseshoe pattern. Stone Age men would have seen 19 of them. Now there are fewer than half that number.

At the very center of Stonehenge, within both the large and small horseshoe formations, the men of ancient times saw a single, towering upright stone. Today it lies flat on the ground. It is called the Altar Stone. If Stonehenge was a religious temple (as many people believe it was), this may have been the place where the high priests held their ceremonies.

Maybe Stonehenge was a place of worship—a place where human sacrifices were made to please pagan gods. But no one really knows.

Today we wonder who brought the stones to the Salisbury Plain; where the stones came from, and how they were transported; and how the stones were cut and shaped, and then erected. We try to determine when Stonehenge was built, and how it looked in ancient times. These are some of the mysteries of Stonehenge. But the greatest mystery of all is, Why? Why did people labor for centuries to build this awesome monument?

For 300 years archeologists have tried to find out why Stonehenge was built—as have anthropologists, engineers, and other scientists. Many astronomers believe that the stones were used to keep track of time, and thus represent a sort of calendar.

In 1960, Gerald Hawkins, an astronomer who came to America from England, became intensely interested in Stonehenge. After years of study, he developed the following theory about why it was built:

The sun was extremely important in the lives of Stone Age people. And so the priests and kings of the tribes would have been much concerned about its coming and going. Anyone who could tell, months ahead, where the sun would appear in the morning or set in the evening would be greatly respected.

Dr. Hawkins reasoned that Stone Age men must have considered the sun and moon to be gods—for they brought good to the
people. The sun created warmth, and the moon lighted the way
at night. When the sun or moon disappeared from the sky, as
during an eclipse, people must have been frightened, thinking

that the gods were displeased and that they were leaving the sky forever. Anyone who could warn the people of such a disaster would naturally hold a position of importance.

Perhaps Stonehenge was intended as a device to tell when there would be an eclipse of the sun or moon.

Dr. Hawkins first studied those eclipses that occurred around the time Stonehenge was built. He figured out where in the sky

the eclipses took place. Then he numbered all the stones as well as the Aubrey Holes and fed these numbers into an electronic computer. The computer matched, wherever possible, the positions and alignments of the stones and holes against the times and locations of the eclipses.

Dr. Hawkins discovered that the 56 Aubrey Holes, just inside the ditch and mound that mark the outer boundary of the Stonehenge site, could be used to predict eclipses. He found that if in 1591 B.C. six stones had been placed in the Aubrey Holes at the

[33]

locations he numbered 56, 47, 38, 28, 19, and 10, and if each stone had been moved to the next hole once a year after that, an important lunar event would have occurred whenever a stone came around to Hole number 56. This is the hole that is situated on a straight line connecting the Heel Stone and the Altar Stone.

In the years between 1591 and 1452 B.C. there were 21 eclipses. At the time of each eclipse, there would have been a stone in Aubrey Hole number 56, had this system been followed. And most of the eclipses would have occurred in a direct line with the Heel Stone.

Since anthropologists know that eclipses have always caused alarm among primitive peoples, it is reasonable to suppose that the design of Stonehenge may be related to happenings in the sky.

Stonehenge might also have been used to predict when the sun would return to a high place in the sky (summer) and bring back once again warmth and plentiful food.

In a six-month period, the place where the sun rises and sets changes a great deal. In summer the sun rises far north of east, and in winter it rises far south of east. Notice carefully where the sun rises or sets today. Then check the location a week or two from now—and you will see that, even in this short time, the sun appears farther north or south, depending upon the season.

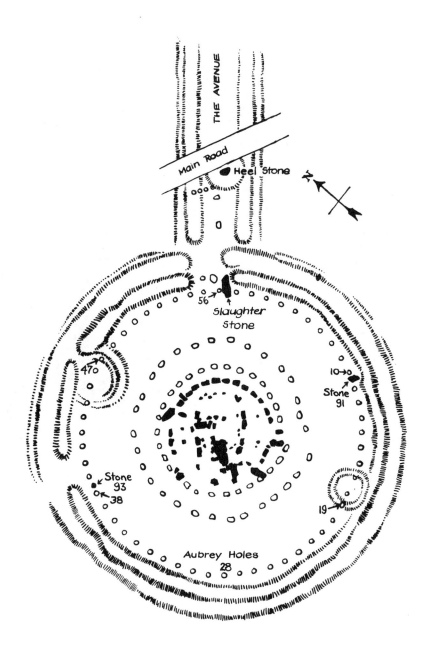

The location where the moon rises and sets also changes a great deal. Within a single month the shift can be from north of the equator to south—the direction, again, depending upon the season of the year.

With great care Dr. Hawkins recorded the positions of the Sarsen Stones and the stones of the inner horseshoe. Then he measured the distances between them and the angles of one stone relative to another. He also figured out where the sun and the moon rose and set over the Salisbury Plain 4,000 years ago. He

gathered hundreds of measurements of the stones and sky positions of the sun and moon. Then the astronomer fed this information into the computer in order to match, wherever possible, the positions and alignments of the stones against the different rising and setting locations of the sun and moon.

Although the computer failed to find a relationship in many cases, it also showed that there were dozens of connections be-

tween the placements of the stones and the events occurring in the sky. One startling example is the following:

If a viewer stood at the center of Stonehenge on February 5 and November 8 and looked over Stone number 91, he would see the sunrise. And if he looked toward Stone number 93 on May 6 and August 8, he would see the sunset.

These four sightings could have been used to mark the passage of the seasons. The beginnings of our seasons of spring and fall are determined by those moments when the sun is directly over the equator. Our summer begins when the sun is at its farthest point north of the equator, and winter starts when the sun is farthest south of the equator. The dates when the four seasons begin are December 21, March 21, June 21, and September 21— or close to them. The dates of sunrise and sunset mentioned in the preceding paragraph are February 5, May 6, August 8, and November 8. Each of these is about 45 days before or after the beginning of our summer or winter. It seems that such a division could not be accidental:

November 8 (44 days before December 21)—
Sunrise above Stone number 91

February 5 (47 days after December 21)—
Sunrise above Stone number 91

May 6 (47 days before June 21)—
Sunset above Stone number 93

August 8 (49 days after June 21)—
Sunset above Stone number 93

The place where the summer sun rises above Stonehenge was also predicted by the computer.

Even today, a person standing on the fallen Altar Stone at the center of Stonehenge can look right through the two pillars of the Sarsen Circle that form the entrance. Beyond the circle he can see the Heel Stone, framed within the space once set off by the two Slaughter Stones. From the viewer's position, the top of the Heel Stone is exactly even with the horizon. On the first day of summer, the rising sun rests momentarily atop the Heel Stone—then continues across the sky. For the people of the Stone Age this day may have been the most important of all. It was the day in each year when the sun reached its highest point in the sky.

Gerald Hawkins and his computer seem to have shown that the stones of Stonehenge are arranged for a definite purpose. It is hard to believe that the large number of occasions when their locations have been related to events in the sky could be accidental.

But astronomers, archeologists, anthropologists, engineers, and nonscientists do not all agree about Stonehenge.

Some think the massive rocks and pillars are the remains of a sacred temple; some believe the monument was built by men of Greek descent who lived in England some three or four thousand years ago; many are convinced that the stones were brought

to the Salisbury Plain from faraway places. But all still wonder why Stonehenge was built at this particular place, and what its purpose could have been. Was it a place of worship? Or was it a calendar that would forewarn the kings and priests of events relating to the sun and moon?

Scientists from around the world have pondered such questions. They have studied the site, using test tubes, microscopes, computers—the many tools of modern science. They have dug into the ground, probed beneath the pillars, explored different avenues to unravel its mysteries. But Stonehenge remains a challenge. Its mysteries may be locked forever within the silent stones.

INDEX

INDEX

age of Stonehenge, 17-20
Altar Stone, 28, 34, 42
astronomy, and Stonehenge, 30-44
Aubrey Holes, 25, 33, 34
Avon River, 8, 20, 22

bluestones, 7, 8, 19, 20, 26

carbon-12, carbon-14, 17-18, 19
charcoal, dating of, 17-18
computer, use of, 33, 38-40
cutting of stones, 8-10

daggers, 1, 21
dating, radiocarbon, 17-18, 19
distance stones hauled, 4, 7-8

eclipses, 31-34

fires, use of, 8

first stage, 18-19

grinding of stones, 10

Hawkins, Gerald, 30-44
Heel Stone, 23, 33, 42
holes (*see also* Aubrey Holes), 12,
        23-25
horseshoes, 26-28, 36

inner ring, 7

lines (for ropes), 5, 6, 13
lintel stones, 4, 10, 14-16, 20, 26,
        28
    method of raising, 14-16

monoliths, 25
moon, and Stonehenge, 36-37
mortise, 10, 14

INDEX

Myceneans, 21-22

number of workers, 7, 20

outer ring, 3

people, Stonehenge, 2-3, 20-22, 30
pillars, 3, 8, 10, 12-16, 20, 22, 23,
    25-28
pottery, 1, 19, 25
purpose of Stonehenge, 22, 28,
    30-47

radiocarbon dating, 17-18, 19
rafts, use of, 8
religious use, 22-23, 28, 30
rings, inner and outer, 3, 7
rollers, use of, 5-7
ropes, *see* lines

Saracens, 25
Sarsen Circle, 25, 42
Sarsen Stones, 25, 36
seasons, and Stonehenge, 38, 42
second stage, 19-20

shaping of stones, 8-10
Slaughter Stone, 23, 42
sledges, 6-7, 8, 16
Stone Age, 18, 21, 22, 23, 30-32,
    42
stones:
    cutting of, 8-10
    distance hauled, 4, 7-8
    grinding of, 10
    setting in place, 12-14
    shaping of, 8-10
    transporting of, 4-8
    weight of, 3, 7
summer, first day of, 42
sun, and Stonehenge, 30-44

tenon, 10
time required for building, 17-20
tools, 1, 8, 12, 16, 25
transporting of stones, 4-8
trilithon, 28

wedges, use of, 10
weight of stones, 3, 7
workers, number of, 7, 20

ABOUT THE AUTHOR

Franklyn M. Branley, Chairman of The American Museum—Hayden Planetarium and consultant on science in elementary education, is well known as the author of many books about astronomy and other sciences for young people of all ages. He wrote *The Mystery of Stonehenge* after a visit to Salisbury Plain to see the ruins firsthand.

Dr. Branley holds degrees from New York University, Columbia University, and the State University of New York College at New Paltz. He lives with his family in Woodcliff Lake, New Jersey.

ABOUT THE ILLUSTRATOR

Victor G. Ambrus lives in England, quite near Stonehenge. He and his family "like anything old and interesting, from Stonehenge to Gothic architecture." Mr. Ambrus notes that his house is a bit like a museum, for it holds his collection of military uniforms and armor; his son's fossils, dinosaur bones, and pre-historic tools; and his wife's antique wax dolls.

Born in Budapest, Mr. Ambrus attended the Hungarian Academy of Fine Art. He left Hungary after the 1956 uprisings and continued his studies at the Royal College of Art in London. While principally a free-lance illustrator, Mr. Ambrus also lectures at the Guildford School of Art in Surrey. He is the illustrator of more than ninety books and in 1965 received the British Library Association's Kate Greenaway Medal for the year's most outstanding illustrated book for children, "The Three Poor Tailors."

Date Due

NO 7 '70	MAR 0 2 1990 MAR 0 2 1990			
MAY 4 '78				
APR 1 9 '79	FEB 2 8 1991			
MAY 1 0 '79				
APR 1 9 1983				
MAY 1 0 1983				
OCT 17 1983				
DEC 17 1987				
2 5				